Cover art by Diana Stumpe

This is a true account of occurrences I experienced while working at Transportation Security Administration .Only the names of the people have been changed, the places and events are accurate. I'm no professional writer, but I've done my best to convey the information in this book.

I worked for TSA for five years. Four of those years were as a lead transportation security officer (LTSO), with over a year of acting supervisor experience. Most of my employment was spent at the Fairbanks International Airport in Alaska with 14 months working at the Deadhorse Airport, which serves Prudhoe Bay Alaska. I saw and reported multiple violations that could be exploited and cause serious harm to the traveling public. Not only was I ignored by local management, but eventually TSA Alaska management dismissed me in an attempt to protect themselves. If you think TSA makes flying safe, it's only because the TSA presence has deterred individuals from even trying. TSA wants their officers to balance security, customer service, efficiency, and speed. However most TSA officers lack some or all of these abilities. With a lackluster workforce, it's no wonder that TSA fails their annual employee tests and upsets the traveling public on a consistent basis.

I0693616

History of TSA failures

TSA has a history of failures, many of these stories can be found by a simple google search, and several are widely known. There was Andy Ramirez who stole an iPad left behind by ABC news and attempted to deny and lie about stealing it. In 2011 over 30 officers and members of management fired from the Honolulu Airport for not screening checked bags. Those people risked thousands of lives because of their laziness. TSA made news again for a 95% fail rate of tests nationwide. Then there was Kelly Hoggan was a top TSA official who received $90,000 in "bonuses" during a 13 month period.

What about the things that don't make the headlines? From video briefings and training videos, i've seen much more of what TSA has to offer. I've seen video footage of baggage officers sleeping on the job, a TSA officer stealing money from a passenger's bag, and a TSA officer and airline baggage handler working together to steal jewelry from bags. There are several accounts of TSA officers helping to smuggle drugs. What if instead of drugs, it had been an explosive device? It only takes one person to look the other, or not perform their job properly and there will be another catastrophic event. After seeing TSA from the inside for five years, I'm amazed that hasn't happened yet.

Chapter 1

Training and Testing

Every TSA officer must go through several weeks of classroom training followed by hours of on the job training for each procedure. Recently TSA centralized the training at Federal Law Enforcement Training Center (FLETC) in Georgia, instead of having each individual airport conduct their own training classes. TSA claims the reason behind this move is to achieve stronger consistency. That feeble excuse was just an expensive smokescreen made to look like TSA is trying to fix their flaws. The FLETC academy only teaches checkpoint screening. Baggage screening is still taught at local airports, by local trainers. Since different airports have different x-rays and explosive detection machines, that means many officers still recieve training by local trainers, and all of the on-job-training is done locally. Training isn't as centralized as they claim.

Have any of you ever had an item taken by TSA that made it through other airports no problem? Some people believe this inconsistency at airports is designed to throw the bad guys off guard. That's not the case. Every airport follows the same set of operating procedures and theoretically should be identical nationwide. The inconsistency comes from bad training, poor management, laziness, and incompetence.

The checkpoint training process at the Fairbanks International Airport is to pair a trainee with a mentor. Not every officer can be a mentor. Management handpicks the officers they deem best suited as trainers and assign them a trainee to coach. One issue in Fairbanks is the small pool of mentors gets burned out from constant training. As soon as a mentor finished with one trainee, a new one would immediately be assigned. This led to TSA management in Fairbanks allowing unqualified officers to become mentors. One such officer was Phil. He was granted mentorship in Fairbanks because of the lack of mentors. Phil not only failed multiple tests requiring him to be remediated, but he also openly mocked and laughed at other officers who failed the same tests. Phil was granted mentorship status by Donna ,the Assistant Federal Security Director, also known as the person in charge of TSA in Fairbanks. Phil's first and only trainee required retraining. Phil was fired from TSA for drug usage.

The Fairbanks airport is hub for thousands of tourists in the summer. During winter there is a significant decrease in passenger throughput. Training hours theoretically only count for procedures actually performed. If a trainee runs the x-ray machine for an hour but does not process any passengers for half that period, then only 30 minutes of actual time should be counted toward the training hours. This isn't always true, as I can confirm first hand.

Near the end of my training, I had only a few hours remaining in the pat down procedure to be completely finished. The lead officer, who was also an assistant trainer had me watch another officer screen passengers at the body scanner, and gave me multiple hours for several minutes of mere observation. How many times around the country, during all the years TSA has existed has this happened? I was prepared to perform my job, but how many times was an officer certified without being properly trained to ensure the nation's safety?

The baggage training process is slightly different. Instead of pairing with a mentor, the officer is trained by whoever happens to be in baggage that day. Baggage training is also done in sections unlike checkpoint training where everything is taught at once. In Fairbanks, when an officer begins baggage training, they only learn bag searches first. X-ray training follows much later, sometimes a year or more. Even though TSA has a set of procedures to follow, each employee does things differently. A trainee being mentored by six different officers isn't going to be trained to the same standards as a person trained by a single mentor.

I informed management that I was only willing to train an officer in baggage if I was the lone mentor. One of my trainees was paired with another mentor when I took a sick day. The other mentor had them perform several procedures incorrectly, all of which went against the TSA operating procedures. Each officer I trained passed the baggage test on their first attempt. Multiple other trainees, all of whom were trained by committee, failed their first attempts. I even watched another trainee for a day who was waiting to take his test. After correcting multiple errors, I informed my manager Dan that he wasn't ready. Dan refused to listen to me. The trainee failed his baggage test twice.

For my own baggage training, is was the same story. I had multiple trainers, each telling me different things, half of them incorrect. A supervisor named Nan made a mistake in the checkpoint and was suspended from screening in the checkpoint. She was moved to baggage screening only for the time. Nan then took over all baggage training during this period. Of course the best choice to train people is somebody who has been decertified in half of the job functions.

While waiting for bags to screen, Nan would ask me questions about checked baggage procedures in an attempt to increase my job knowledge. Most of the time I would answer, she look confused. She would then flip through our copy of the standard operating procedures for verification. Nan didn't even know the answers to questions she asked me, and yet she was the mentor.

When I received my first trainee, the training department also warned me about his behavior. He was constantly late to class, he fell asleep in class, and he never dressed or acted in a professionally. After two weeks of multiple warnings and continued infractions, most companies would accept the loss and let the employee go. TSA however prefers to keep the bad performers and hope they magically change. I trained him for four weeks. He was constantly late, half-asleep, his uniform was a crumpled mess and he often reeked of drugs. I informed management of behavior on multiple occasions but they were not interested. After four weeks of him showing no improvement in the screening operations, TSA finally decided to let him go.

He was not the only officer in Fairbanks that they kept and hoped for the best. Fairbanks can't be the only airport that has practiced this, so it's safe to say TSA has wasted hundreds of thousands of dollars of taxpayer money simply because they don't want to take the time to recruit other candidates.

Fairbanks TSA does have a good explosive expert by the name of Glenn, who attempts to train the officers. Every month Glenn creates test bags with common items that can be used to hide bomb components and show it to the officers. When Glenn runs his covert tests, TSA officers miss his items at an alarming rate. The troubling part is not when he runs covert, but when he the officers are aware he's around. Glenn will bring two or three bags with different items and take a group of two to four officers to an X-ray machine and ask them what they see. A few officers will spot some of the dangerous items in the bag, but others start to make things up, seeing imaginary threats, because they can't identify the real item.

Glenn will sometimes use members of the armed services as undercover role players pretending to be passengers. Glenn gives the role players various scenarios to test the officers. One such event occurred when I was about three months into the job. The scenario was as follows. A passenger had an item that looked similar to explosive in his bag. A search was called on the item. The supervisor at the time, Francine, who has been with TSA for 10 years at this point, and working airport security for several years prior, responded to conduct the search. When Francine tested the bag for explosives, the machine alarmed, confirming traces of explosive residue. The role player immediately fled the area and returned to the ticket counter, which is outside the security one. Francine is left holding an item that alarmed for explosive, with the passenger dashing off in a hurry.

Francine began walking around in circles, her face a mask of confusion. Francine gave no instruction to any officer as she wandered aimlessly. Obviously, Francine failed the test, as drifting around with an explosive in your hand and doing zilch is the incorrect procedure.

Glenn also conducts classroom training. One course he taught was advanced smuggling. He covered five different methods in which people attempt to smuggle items. When the course was over, a male officer was to give him a pat down. I was chosen to perform the pat down and began finding the items, each hidden using a different smuggling technique he covered in class.

When class was finished, he told me that I was the first officer to find all five items, and when all classes were completed, only two out of six officers found all five items. TSA Fairbanks had a 67%

fail rate, despite the fact the officers had just sat through the class.

TSA holds annual testing for all officers to ensure standards are met. While this idea is good in theory, TSA has dumbed down testing to avoid officers failing. When I started at TSA, the testing consisted of an X-ray image assessment, a standard operating procedure assessment or SOPA, and a physical search portion, which consisted of two pat downs and three bag searches. If an officer fails any of the tests, they are put into remediation for that area and required to retest. If an officer fails a test three times, they are fired. In the last five years, at least two officers were fired from the Fairbanks airport for failing a test three times.

Testing season began six months after I started TSA. First up was the SOPA. Since it was computer a based test, multiple officers could take it at the same time. During the shift briefing, all the officers were asked who would like to take the test first. The week before testing began, the senior officers talked about being afraid to take the test. Naturally nobody volunteered to go first. Matt, an officer who went through new hire class with me, and I were then chosen to go first. It turned out that the SOPA was just a multiple choice job knowledge test, and was extremely easy. Despite how easy the test was, multiple officers failed. An officer can't perform any functions related to the area of the test they failed. Three years ago, TSA stopped administering the SOPA, because of the huge inconvenience of officers failing. We can all feel safer knowing TSA doesn't require an annual job knowledge test anymore.

The pat down and bag search tests have dumbed down as well. In the past, TSA would give all five tests at once and be done. It was considered too stressful to test officers this way. In reality, too many officers were failing. Now the tests are distributed throughout the year, and officers can take multiple practice test until they get it right before taking the real test. This way officers don't score fails on the actual test and less of them that can't do the job are fired. With multiple practices to get it right, TSA can also report a higher testing rate.

The most TSA friendly thing about the new testing method if an officer is sick or tired and thinks they won't do well on the test, no problem, the test can be rescheduled for another day. The officer can continue screening people and property after claiming to be sick or tired. Hows that for a new TSA motto, not fit to test, real thing is no problem.

Another method TSA uses to attempt to keep officers skills up is called the Threat Image Projection System or TIPS. TIPS is fake computer generated images such as bombs, guns and knives placed in the X-ray image of a bag. If an officer scores under 75% TIPs caught for a month, they are placed on remediation and have to be mentored on the X-ray machine for a short time. It's sad that the pass percentage is that low. I understand no officer is getting a 100% score every month. TSA is fine with the officers missing 25% of the threats. However if that percentage was higher, more officers would fail, and that would require TSA to train officers better. An investment TSA would rather not make.

When an officer thinks they see a TIP, they hit the search button on the X-ray machine. If a TIP is present a message will pop up saying you caught the TIP and the image will disappear. If no TIP was in the bag, a message will pop up saying there was no TIP in the image and a loud audible beep can be heard. The pressure to pass leads to a bigger problem in TSA. If an officer see what they think is a TIP, they hit the button. Many times, if not TIP is present, the officer will let the bag continue with no further screening.

Think about this for a moment. A TSA officer thinks they saw a computer generated threat. When they realize it's not fake, they allow it through instead of visually viewing the real item. I have seen this happen dozens if not hundreds at TSA in Fairbanks alone.

Another issue is that officers often get excited and brag about finding computer generated items, and will halt the screening process, in order to show other officers what they found.

In 2016, Ryan, the Federal Security Director or FSD of Alaska, sent an email to all Alaska TAS employees about the TIP system. The email was in regards to the remediation process of the TIPS program. The email explained the pass percentage, the mentoring process, and the need for remediation as many officers were confused about the process. The email then went on to show statistics of the TIP program in Alaska through the first eight months of that year. The officers at the Anchorage airport had over 200 TIP remediations, while the rest of the airports in Alaska had thirteen combined. The Anchorage staff cannot accurately spot threats on the X-ray. A comforting thought.

This email also has another message Ryan probably didn't consider. If Ryan had to send the email to every Alaska employee, it means many officers were confused and didn't understand the remediation process. What this email is unintentionally saying, the Anchorage airport has not been performing the remediation process for who knows how long, and has been contributing to the mediocrity that is TSA.

TSA has a large supply of simulated explosive and bomb components, each contained in separate ziplock bags. Officers can put these items into bags to assist with training, or run covert drills on each other. When I was a new hire, the drills were run every day, over time they decreased until they became nonexistent. One day while working in baggage, the checkpoint supervisor asked me to make a drill bag and run in on the X-ray machine. When most officers run the drill bag, they leave the items in the ziplock bags and spread them around to make it harder to see. This time I decided to remove all the items, and assemble them into a mock bomb. I placed the bag on the x-ray belt during a busy time, without the operator seeing, and waited for the officer to find the bomb. About a minute later, the drill bag is at the end of the table, where passengers can pick up their cleared property. I quickly grabbed the bag and informed the supervisor that the X-ray officer just let a fully assembled bomb onto an airplane. The supervisor was uninterested, and the officer was allowed to continue screening with zero training or remediation. This event shows that TSA officers are undertrained, not held accountable for their mistakes, and leadership is unwilling to correct the issues to make TSA effective.

TSA forbids officers from making physical contact with any person who goes through security without being screened. Any crazed person could run, or just leisurely stroll past the TSA officers and carry out an attack on the passengers who already cleared security. What are TSA officers allowed to do? They can say stop, they can trail the individual, and they can call police. While TSA is pretending to be security, a gunman or bomber could easily carry out an attack on hundreds of travelers with no cover and no chance to escape.

When passengers are considered high risk, but haven't made the no fly list, they are called a selectee. Selectees have an extra marking on their boarding pass that is easily recognizable by TSA, or at least it's supposed to be. Selectees receive the highest level of screening, and missing a selectee is a big deal at TSA. Such a big deal that an officer in Fairbanks was fired after missing one. The problem is nationwide, with countless selectees not screened to standards. Boarding passes differ from airline to airline, but they all have the same basic information. The selectee marking is large and bold, and an officer seeing hundreds or thousands of boarding passes a day should notice the extra marking. This highlights the laziness and lack of awareness by TSA officers to find something they are trained to look for. If TSA is having trouble noticing a large mark on a piece of paper, then what items could go missed in a bag with dozens of other items concealing it?

Chapter 2

Leadership and other roles

I was promoted to lead officer after a year at TSA. My promotion was even as shady as the rest of TSA operations. The lead opening was posted for ten days. Five days before the application time period closed, Cameron, the Assistant Federal Security Director called me into a meeting. Cameron asked me if I had applied for the lead opening. After I told him that I had, he offered me the spot. Cameron hadn't reviewed any applications or conducted interviews.

I wasn't the only person in Fairbanks that was promoted this way, as it happened multiple times over the years. Fairbanks isn't the only airport that uses this practice. TSA management makes it a practice to show favoritism, and i'm sure many qualified and hard working officers were passed over because of their biased nature.

At TSA, there is no official training process when officers are promoted. I was sent to Dead Horse, which has two terminals, often requiring me to be acting supervisor. My supervisor, Nil, did a great job of training me. If my supervisor would have been somebody, like Francine for example, I would have learned absolutely nothing. Later I realized that Nil only ensured I was trained so that she would have less to do. I often did her paperwork while she was playing candy crush on her phone. Many times, if there was only one flight, Nil would send all the officers to work while she stayed in the office. Nil was probably playing video games, as she also had her Xbox in the office as well.

I attended lead training at FLETC two years after I was promoted. The two weeks training course was a joke. We covered how to talk to different employees without hurting their feelings, and were shown a history of terrorist attacks. One instructor often looked confused, and whenever he would forget what he was saying, he would walk over to the poster with the TSA mission statement and just point at it.

For an hour of the two weeks we were there, we went to a mock airport for training. We were separated into groups of three, with leads from the other classes, to work with people we haven't met. We were given scenarios and took turns handling situations and rating each other. In one scenario, I was the observer. A roleplayer was acting as a passenger watching his checked bag being screened. He used an irate tone and asked the lead questions about the screening process, including how would the lead handled his property. The lead officer responded, "since you're here, I'll repack everything neatly". His use of 'since your here' got a response from the roleplayer. He asked "what would you do if I wasn't here?". The lead had no answer and just stood there with a look of shock on his face.

The entire training was a waste of time and money, as all leads from around the entire country would eventually be required to go. The leads in my class often asked stupid questions, like my favorite, "why doesn't the metal detector pick up nonmetal items?".

In close second was when the Hawaii lead asked me if I had a layover in Hawaii on my way back to Alaska. My guess it this came up because maps often depict Alaska near Hawaii, and if one is an island, the other must also be an island.

One of the most important job aspects of TSA leadership is to resolve screening alarms. When TSA officers search through bags, or pat people down, you will see they use a small cloth, to wipe their hands, the passengers' hands, and some property. Then they place the cloth into a machine and it checks if any traces of explosives are present on the cloth. If the machine detects explosive traces, it will make a loud beeping noise and print out a piece of paper with the details of what type of explosive it picked up and some other information. The print out has lots of numbers displayed, but only a few are required to resolve the alarm. Most officers, including leadership, have no idea what each number means, and they repeatedly look at the wrong numbers, which means they don't actually clear the explosive alarm. Of course that is only if the supervisor even bothers to look at the paper, which doesn't always happen. As long at TSA does it right five percent of the time, then they consider themselves the gold standard of security screening.

A lead or supervisor must always be present at the checkpoint during screening. Many supervisors in Fairbanks leave the checkpoint to "do supervisor work" often leaving the lead stuck in the checkpoint and doing all the work. Several times this happened to me, I would call the supervisor or lead from baggage area to cover the checkpoint for a few minutes. Then I would find the checkpoint supervisor lounging in the break room. When the supervisor would see me, they would say, oh I did this and this and that, and I just took a break and I was about to come back so you could take a break. It's interesting that every time this happened, whether it was 30 minutes or two hours after they left they were "about to come back".

You can't expect TSA to perform well when even the head of TSA refuses to do anything useful. I believe it was summer of 2012, when Administrator Pistol came to Fairbanks to speak to TSA employees. During the hour long meeting, he wasted 30 minutes telling stories about his family. For the Q&A period, I planned to asked about the terrible condition of the national deployment force (NDF), which I will address later. He ignored my hand, and only took the pre submitted questions, which he had handy cards to help answer the approved inquiries.

Feeling frustrated, I emailed Admin Pistol about the many failures of TSA and asked what he was doing to address it. My email was never answered. However, during his visit, he gave his email to a female officer, and told her say hi sometime. Administrator Pistol did return the email of the female officer writing hello and asking how she was doing. It's very reassuring to know that the former administrator of TSA was using hundreds of thousands of dollars to fly around the country gathering female officers' emails and ignoring the issues of TSA. When Neffenger took office, I emailed him as well, but I never received a reply from him either.

Every year, supervisors write performance reviews for their assigned officers. Getting a high enough score on the reviews leads to raises and bonuses for the officers. The supervisor then submits the review to a manager to approve or change as the manager see fit. The supervisor then meets with the officer to discuss the review. At least two supervisors, Nil and KB, both used copy paste on reviews but forgot to change the name of the officer. This resulted in one officer's name appearing in the review of another officer. This of course shows they took spent no effort and unfairly scored some officers. Of course the managers are to blame as well, as Dan and Dick were not reading the reviews, just approving them with quick glances.

When the supervisors conducts reviews, they put on these huge acts how long the reviews take to complete and they need the leads to handle their workload. I can't imagine all the effort it took to copy and paste the reviews. KB also rated hispanic officers lower in communication because as he put it "English isn't their first language".

Every six months Fairbanks has a shift bid where officers bid based on seniority for shifts and days off. An officer's rating supervisor is usually the supervisor they work with most. A week before shift bid, the shifts were released so officers could began planning what their preferences.

AJ, a lead officer that we will discuss in more depth later, was universally disliked. As the senior male lead, I was slotted to bid first, with AJ bidding second. There were two spots on the night schedule for male leads. Francine was the last of supervisors to bid. As the supervisor's already had their bids in, Francine knew what schedule she would be working. One lead spot mirrored her schedule exactly, while the other was opposite. Francine offered to give me perfect ratings if I would work the same days as her. She really didn't want to work with AJ. Of course this is a violation as the rating are performance based and not rewarded for agreeing with a supervisor. I reported this to Dan.

About a year later, I overheard Francine talking about two leads that switched shifts, a new lead, Stoak was switching with Steffon to match her schedule. Francine was upset over having Stoak working with her. She made the comment "well Steffon just lost out on a perfect rating". I assume she attempted to make the same deal with Steffon to avoid working with Stoak. I again reported this to Dan, and he still did nothing. Supervisors can use the rating system to reward or punish officers, and management does nothing to address this issue. Francine can't be only supervisor in TSA history to use ratings this way.

TSA has an additional screening process called playbook. Playbook teams conduct extra screening at various location in the airport, such as screening airport employees using access doors, passengers at gates, and sometimes before the security checkpoint. Have you ever noticed two or three officers standing at the gate on theirs phones? That's the playbook team not working. As I will mention later, I have seen this on multiple occasions.

There are many other roles in TSA besides the screening officers.TSA also has canine handlers. In the rare effort to save money instead of spend, the canine handlers in Fairbanks were disbanded. In the three years that I worked "alongside" the handlers, I only ever saw them conduct screening on one occasion. Just about every time they came to the airport, instead of sniffing for explosives, they were training when no passengers were present. While I understand the need for training is important, the canine handlers never performed the job they were being paid to do.

Another role is the behavior detection officer (BDO). These officers stand near the lines and are trained to read behaviors from people to determine threats. To TSA the BDO may sound like a good program, and TSA can use it to claim they are attempting smart security, but the behavior officers themselves make it a joke. In Fairbanks, the BDOs were never at the checkpoint during the busy periods, but would show up during slow times and talk to other officers. Since they were under a different chain of command, they would get away with doing little real work.

Behavior officers assumed they could boss around the screening officers. The majority of screening officers have shoulder boards with a single stripe, lead officers have two stripes, and supervisors have three stripes. The stripes are misleading. Officers who become training instructors also receive two or three stripes, the same goes for BDOs. The stripes don't designate rank, but rather pay band. For instance, when our three stripe training instructor would come to the checkpoint to screen, he would ask what I, a two stripe lead, who like him to do. He understood the chain of command in screening.

Many BDOs do not understand this concept. They try to order officers around and get into conflict with actual leadership. The problem was so intense, that the TSA forum called Idea Factory made a monthly challenge to bridge the gap between screeners and BDOs. One BDO shared his comments on the idea factory which perfectly summed up their beliefs. He wrote that while he was in the military, if a ranking officer from any branch gave you an order, you followed it. He went to suggest TSA should be the same. He wrote "if I give an order to any one stripe officer, they should have to follow it", this is the narrow minded thinking that fuels the problems.

Supervisors and leads are promoted in the leadership path: BDOs are not. In fact BDOs do not take any form of leadership training, and lose just about all their screening certifications. Yet, they believe they can order around the screeners simply because they have one more stripe on their shoulder.

Another role in TSA is called the coordination center (CC). These officers are behind the scenes sitting at computers. Their job functions include but are not limited to, taking sick calls, providing support during incidents, and copy/pasting the supervisor's daily paperwork and incident reports into the national database.

The CC is open 24 hours, seven days a week. The Fairbanks airport closes down for several hours each night. When arriving for my morning shift, I witnessed the CC officer lounging in the break room watching TV, instead of working in his office. The worst part is that it's a grown man watching a Justin Bieber music video. The same officer would also steal lunches from the refrigerator, including my own on one occasion. Fairbanks management did nothing to address this issue thus allowing theft in the workplace.

Back to the NDF. The officers in the NDF are called national deployment officers (NDO). The NDOs are sent wherever needed throughout the year. They may be sent to Alaska in the summer and Hawaii in the winter. One major problem with the NDF program is that every airport maintains different types of equipment. The NDOs are not trained and certified on every machine. Officers placed in Fairbanks can't perform many of the job functions and can often be a hindrance rather than a help, such as requiring a local officer to operate equipment for them, thus defeating the purpose of spending millions of dollars on NDO travel and salary. If the local officers are busy, then the passengers screened by the NDO have to wait.

One NDO supervisor named Neo, while giving a briefing on his first day in Fairbanks stated "NDOs are the best of the best, the highest rated officers". The NDOs however have proven quite the opposite. Of the dozens of NDOs that have come to Fairbanks over the years, only one was actually good.

On the same day Neo claimed his people are the best ever, another NDO supervisor asked me if the 16 oz syrup bottle he was holding was allowed through. As many people are aware, the allowed limit is 3.4oz, and best of the best should know that 16 is higher than 3.4. I told the item was too large to be allowed through the checkpoint, and he replied "but it's in a ziplock bag", as if that somehow allowed the rules to changed. I said again, it's over 3.4oz and can't go, he responded with "oh okay, I was just checking how you do things here". How we do things here, the SOP is the same for the entire country, going so far as to require TSA in Alaska to call the police for certain knives because they are illegal in other states. This NDO supervisor has been allowing prohibited items through at other airports, as have the many other officers around the country. This causes anger and confusion when TSA takes an item at one airport that was allowed through at others.

Neo once allowed a passenger who had alarmed for explosives to board his flight with no additional screening. The best of the best himself, allowed a passenger with a positive explosive test to board an airplane and fly away without even asking him a single question. On another occasion, as I returned from lunch, an officer approached me about a procedure Neo was doing incorrectly. He was sure Neo was incorrect, but wanted my opinion. I was able to step in and correct Neo, however, if I had not come back at that time, this officer would have allowed the incorrect procedure. Many officers are afraid to confront supervisors when the violate procedure, and allow the violation to continue.

The list on NDO discretions is a long one, so I will tackle it from earliest to most recent. One NDO left the metal detector without telling anyone, and didn't rope it off. Anybody with non metal bomb parts could have walked right through the Fairbanks airport and nobody would notice. The NDO was later discovered hiding in the bathroom while eating a candy bar

Another NDO did a bag search I called from X-ray on a full size toothpaste, clearly over the 3.4oz size limit. Several minutes later he was back by the X-ray with no items. At the time, all bags had to be sent through the X-ray a second time after it was searched. Not only did he fail to perform the correct procedure, but he allowed a prohibited item through screening. I called a supervisor who had locate the passenger and retrieve the toothpaste.

As mentioned before, the screening process for checked baggage is a bit different. One shift, I was working with a NDO lead, and another officer who was not certified on the X-ray, but could do searches when directed by a certified X-ray operator. I was searching a bag, when the NDO asked me if I would call a search on the bag currently alarming X-ray. When I looked at the image,every item in the bag had to be searched according to the SOP. The NDO probably would have let the items through had the other officer not seem the image. It was clear it would be a considerable amount of work, and he didn't want to do it.

Most passengers go through the body scanner where they hold perfectly still with their arms above their head. The machine has a screen that shows yellow boxes of areas where the machine thinks items could be hidden. The officer has to pat down those areas to ensure nothing is there. I witnessed one NDO barely tap a passenger to clear a large yellow box. This person could have had 10 dvds strapped to them, and the NDO would have been clueless. After the officer allowed the passenger to continue, I went to the passenger and explained the mistake and I did the proper screening. I took this issue to management, but as usual, nothing was done about it. The NDOs are also rude to passengers, saying things such as "this isn't a grocery store, move" to people getting their items out for X-ray screening.

During my first trip to Deadhorse, there was an officer from Anchorage telling stories about when he was a NDO. He claimed he was partying with famous people in Las Vegas and other outlandish things. To become a NDO, each airport approves or denies its local officers that apply. The day after he told his stories, he ranted about the program, saying only the worst officers were selected because airports wanted to get rid of their lowest performers. Given what i've seen, this statement seems to be mostly true. The best part however was he was completely oblivious to the fact he putting himself in the category.

As mentioned before TSA has a shift bid every six months. For the state of Alaska, 90% of the scheduling officer's job is copy pasting the previous schedule to the new schedule. He apparently has so much work that TSA gave him an assistant. So TSA Alaska is paying $100,000 plus for two people to copy and paste every six months.

Let's delve more into the Idea Factory. The Idea Factory is a forum in which TSA employees can post, comment, and rate ideas. Nothing shows the mass stupidity of an organization like reading ideas from the employees. Many of the posts are repeated to death, because most people are incapable of original thinking. One popular idea was arming TSA officers. Next time you're at the airport, look at the TSA officers and imagine all of them with a firearm. How many of them would you trust? Most people suggested only arming the supervisors, which is still a terrible idea. In Fairbanks alone, Nil's hand constantly shakes, and she takes all kinds of medication. Francine would mostly likely have her firearm taken from her by somebody with ill intentions. If somehow she managed to draw and fire, she would mostly likely shoot a TSA employee or innocent passenger, rather than an active shooter.

One officer suggested that TSA should have no leadership and each officer should handle their own situation, schedule their own workload and breaks, and who ever wants to can do the paperwork. With no supervision, who would hold people accountable for their actions?

In Fairbanks, most people want the same lunch time. So if every person picks their own lunch, then TSA will just close down whenever the officers feel like it. What if nobody wants to check bags? Do the officers all stand around until end of shift? It's ridiculous that a government employee who the public has to trust with their life thinks this would be a good idea. I would bet the person is incapable of even thinking through the above consequences, which makes it that more ridiculous.

One of the worst ideas come from a Fairbanks officer. The idea stated that officers in Alaska should be issued snuggies because it's cold. Nothing says professional security like a snuggie.

Chapter 3

Fairbanks operations

I have witnessed so many violations in Fairbanks over my five years.I will start with earliest events and then continue with same violations from those people. When I was first hired in November of 2011, the FSD Jasper, was already under investigation for sexual harassment, and was soon let go. Two supervisors were then fired for sexual harassment. This was all during the first two weeks I worked for TSA.

Some incidents are so common that they cover most of the officers, multiple times. Many officers are much worse at X-ray screening then they believe themselves to be. Since most officers have terrible item recognition, they will call searches on common items, such as apples, bananas, laser pointers, keys and end up slowing down the entire screening process.

At the time I left TSA, at least 50% of the Fairbanks officers had missed prohibited Items such as knives, tasers, fireworks, and bullets. Many of these items I happened to notice, but how many passed through undiscovered. That's just the dangerous items. I've found liquids, pool cues, and other items TSA prohibits from getting on the aircraft. TSA is inconsistent when officers miss items. In several cases the officer was required to take X-ray remediation, other times the supervisor never even speaks to the officer. TSA has no problem with mediocrity and officers won't improve if not held accountable for their mistakes.

Some of the following details aren't violations, but shows the level of officer stupidity and how frustrating it is to deal with as an employee or passenger. Look up the Mad TV wheel of fortune skit with David Arquette. The contestants are an accurate representation of TSA officers.

The first officers to get fired after I started TSA, besides the ones mentioned above, committed baggage screening violations similar to those in Hawaii. It was a team of officers at the Deadhorse airport, all of whom were based out of Fairbanks. Unlike the Hawaii incident, this one didn't make headlines. Seven of the eight officers were fired because they conducted no screening on the checked baggage. Since Deadhorse doesn't have an X-ray for checked baggage, all bags have to be opened and inspected by TSA. These officers were too lazy to do their job properly. The eighth officer was the supervisor and was spared because instead of working, the supervisor was sitting in the office doing no work, and claimed she didn't know it was happening.

The first violation I personally witnessed was while working the front tables helping people take the proper items out of their bags. As the scanner will detect items left in pockets, I informed the passengers to remove all items from their pockets. One gentlemen pulled a knife out of his pocket asked me what to do. I informed him the item needed to go through the X-ray since his property has already started through. I told him an officer would help him once he was done with the screening process. I put the knife in a bowl by itself, and told the X-ray operator the knife was coming through. Several minutes later the lead officer asked what I know about the knife. I told him that I placed it in the bowl and told the X-ray operator it was coming through. He then told me that the knife was on the exit table where passengers repack their property. The X-ray operator was an older woman who had started only a few months before me. She let the knife, which had no other items to obstruct the view go through to the secure area.

The next time I worked with her was in Deadhorse during my first rotation up. The supervisor had a phone meeting with management during a flight. The lead officer also decided to join the meeting. With no leadership on site we were violating TSA policy, but they told us to carry on anyway. The supervisor of was Nil, no surprise there. Anyway, the knife lady was on X-ray. I was at the search table changing gloves when all of the sudden, she was next to me grabbing gloves. I looked to the passengers, with no X-ray operator, the line wasn't moving. I asked her what she was doing, and she replied "well I kept missing the TIPs that showed up so I took myself off". She did this without telling anybody, but if she missed every fictional item, then what real items did she let through? She was fired about six months later.

On the same Deadhorse rotation, there was an Anchorage officer who really stood out. There were two events that make me question how he could possibly work as a security officer with people's lives in his hands. One day he was checking driver's licenses, while I was operating the metal detector. The screening checkpoints in Deadhorse are small rooms. The ID checker is located outside the room at the door. Halfway through the screening process, he leans through the door and asks me for batteries for the UV light that is used to check IDs. I told the lead officer, who then begins to look for them. About a minute later, he leans in again saying nevermind, he got it. The UV flashlight was the twist handle, so I assumed he just tightened it and got it working again. When most of the passengers were through, and we were waiting for a few stragglers, I looked out the door, and he was holding a regular flashlight. The entire time he was shining a ordinary light. Obviously no UV features on the IDs were showing, but he allowed the passengers through anyway.

The second event happened when he was operating the X-ray machine and I was the search officer. He was looking at a bag for a minute so I went over and asked if there I was something he wanted me to look at. He said "no, I just couldn't tell if this was an electric razor, or a toothpaste". These items are completely different. There's no mistaking the items on X-ray. They appear as different colors, and a razor is made up of multiple tiny parts while toothpaste is a clumped mass. When I looked at the screen, it was clearly a razor. I'm not sure if he actually had trouble telling the items apart, or if that's the best story he could come up with on the spot, either way, he made an idiot of himself.

One officer by the name of RJ didn't last long. Before Fairbanks stopped conducting the random screening of playbook, I ended up scheduled on playbook with him twice. Instead of screening, he only wanted to sit on the bench by the window to cover the unloading area. When he was unable to sit all night, he would complain like a child. RJ got fired when he was checking IDs. He had his back to the waiting line of passengers while he stared at a flight attendant. He was looking away so long that people got tired of waiting and starting walking passed him. When the FSD asked him for a statement regarding his side of the story, he wrote cheeseburgers.

If any employee, it doesn't matter where you work, has an entire list of local policies created because of them, they probably shouldn't work there any more. At TSA Fairbanks that employee is Barry. Barry has worked at TSA since they in Alaska. If I had worked with Barry for his entire career, I would probably have a Barry stand alone trilogy.

I've heard many stories from before I worked with him, and while i'm sure most if not all are true, we'll stick the the ones I witnessed. The first time I worked with Barry when was I was still in training. My monitor was a lead officer. When he was scheduled for baggage, I was also in baggage, even though I hadn't had baggage training yet. I was payed for ten hours of work to help lift heavy bags when needed, and complete a few online training courses. I was sitting by the baggage X-ray when Barry, while talking on the phone, walked into the emergency stop button, shutting down the baggage entire belt.

When assigned to the body scanner, Barry would constantly walk away without telling his partner. His partner, assuming Barry was at his post, allowed passengers through. This cause problems on multiple occasions as uncleared passengers walked off. We had to track them down and bring them back, making sure they didn't hand any items off to other people or hide them somewhere.

Barry loves to talk probably more than anything. He would talk to everybody, even if they completely ignored him. He would leave his assigned post to follow passengers to talk with them. One time, having found out a passenger was a doctor, Barry lifted him sleeve to expose his arm so he could ask the doctor's opinion on a rash. He once talked to another officer for 10 minutes about cats, the only thing the other officer said was "I don't like cats". He repeated about 30 times, to which Barry was oblivious. To be fair, the conversation would have ended sooner, but I decided to egg Barry on and said "Barry, I bet if you talk about cats more, he will start to like them". That of course was all Barry needed to talk more about cats.

Barry often allowed passengers pressure him to attempt to keep oversized liquids. He would ask if this item or that item was okay because a little bit was used. I lost track of the times I hold Barry, half an ounce used doesn't turn a 12oz liquid into and 3.4oz liquid.

Barry is also the very dishonest. For every little injury, he attempts to claim workers' compensation. He filed a claim for leg cramps, and the TSA injury claims hotline operator just laughed and hung up on him. I asked Barry why he always tried and he said he didn't expect to win any of the claims. Barry told me he was hoping that somebody messed up the paperwork, and he would win his claim by default. All Barry wants is for somebody to forget to sign a paper, and he can sit at home with his paper cut collecting a paycheck.

When assigned to the ticket check, he would constantly wander over the snowmachine video display 50 feet away. Passengers would then walk up and wait because he's watching ads or moving signs around. The best way to describe Barry in the workplace would be as a pinball. He bounces around randomly with no thought or direction and needs to constantly be pushed to regain his course. Barry had so many violations, that he was placed on a performance improvement plan, which means he has to be watched during every screening process.

Barry is that person that will ask every stupid question. Every two years, all airport employees are assigned new security access badges. Each employee must go to the badging office. When it was time to get new badges, the supervisors would inform the officers during briefing. Barry once asked "where do we go to get the badges?". A valid question for a new officer, not a ten year veteran. Nil responded to him "the same place it's been the last ten years". I somehow managed to get stuck with Barry in just about every classroom training course. Every single class, he would ask questions when we were just given the information. He often had a hard time understanding lessons, when nobody else was confused.

Officer Leb is a female Barry. Leb once found drugs while conducting a search in checked baggage. The drugs were of course confiscated by the airport police. When the passenger took TSA to court over the drug discovery Leb was called to testify. When she took the stand, she couldn't properly explain how or why she conducted the search. Which of course brings up the question, was she conducting the search legally to begin with? The passenger was given his illegal drugs back, because Leb is an idiot.

Leb was also stationed with Barry at the scanner when both of them walked away at the same time, allowing uncleared passengers to walk through. One night Leb was stationed at the metal detector when a dog was coming through. The search officer at the time, normally the officer who would conduct the explosive test, is allergic to dogs, so he stayed far away from the dog as possible. I was at X-ray looking at images when Leb said "it's okay, it's a cat". I look up to see an elderly woman standing three feet in front of Leb. The woman is barely holding a 30 plus pound dog, way larger than any house cat could ever be. I started laughing at how stupid this scenario was. I wasn't the only one, other passengers are laughing as well at the stupidity of TSA, an organization that can't tell a cat from a dog If TSA believes dogs are cats, it's no wonder they harass the elderly and handicapped, as they believe them to be terrorists.

Leb had a moment where I almost snapped at her. At TSA breaks are 15 minutes long. As a lead officer is was my job create a daily schedule where each officer is stationed for each 30 minute period and assign breaks and lunches. One night Leb looks at the schedule, which had her going break at that very minute. She looks at me and asks “when do you want me to go to break?”. As we both know I have her scheduled for now the question seems rather stupid, but I let it go and told her to go now. She followed it up with stupid question number two, “how long is the break?”. I responded “15 minutes, like always”. Just when I thought it was over, stupid question number three comes out of nowhere, “when do you want me to come back?”. I did my best to hide my frustration, and said in a somewhat sarcastic tone “in 15 minutes”, I did manage to contain the, are you fucking stupid part, that I wanted to say, as I most likely would have been fired.

One night after work, since it was 30 degrees below zero, I started my car and was waiting for it to warm up. While waiting, I was sitting on a bench by the door talking to my friend who was also waiting for his car to warm up. The time is 2am and the airport is completely shut down. Leb walked past us and went out the door on her way to her car. She only took a few steps outside and realized the two of us were going nowhere and she could talk our ears off. She came back in and started talking to us even though we were in the middle of a conversation. She kept talking despite the fact we never even acknowledged she was there. Finally I said that it’s cold by the door, and my friend and myself move away from the door. Leb followed and kept talking the entire time. I decided to go the bathroom, followed by my friend. Of course neither of us needed to go, we justed wanted to get away from Leb. Leb followed us to the bathroom, talking the entire way. She was so caught up in talking, that she almost walked into the mens bathroom. She talked into the bathroom the whole time we hid there. Her screeching echoing off the walls. The CIA should consider hiring Barry and Leb for interrogations. An hour locked in a room with these two, and anybody would sell out their own mother to escape.

The baggage area can get loud with the X-rays, moving belts, and other machines continuously humming in an enclosed space. Management eventually purchased sets of ear plugs for baggage officers to help with the noise levels. One shift, while working with Leb in baggage, I decided to use the earplugs to drown out her constant clucking. While not completely noise canceling, I did receive some relief.

One day Leb was complaining about congress rejecting a half percent raise for TSA. She said "that's $3,000 a year out of my pocket." TSA and math, they don't go together. Leb used to be a NDO before Fairbanks staffing levels got low and required her to stay. If somebody as clueless as Leb can make into the program, the best of the best don't seem very good after all.

While Barry and Leb are stupid, and probably don't suck at their job on purpose, officer Flair is not only incompetent, but just plain lazy. Flair would purposely skip screening steps because she didn't want to do the work. If I noticed the violations, I would make her perform the correct procedures, often as she feigns ignorance. The fact that Flair would purposely cause violations should have led to her firing long ago. Flair committed what's probably the worst violation I've ever witnessed, and I will cover that later.

The above three officers rank second, third, and fourth for worst officers in Fairbanks. They are lazy, incompetent, and dishonest. AJ ranks number one. AJ actually knows most of the procedures, and isn't slow as hell like many others. What sets AJ apart is that he's a bloodthirsty backstabber, that will purposely allow an officer to commit a violation just to get them in trouble. AJ thinks he is TSA, and everybody else is below him.

You can't mention AJ without mentioning his lapdog Steffon. AJ is an asshole that nobody wants to be around. Steffon is socially awkward, doesn't shower, and has low self esteem. They make a perfect pair for a controlling type friendship, as nobody else wanted anything to do with them. They would coordinate their sick calls, leave their duty stations to talk, and often talked instead of focusing on work.

My second time to Deadhorse, I worked on a team with AJ, Steffon, and a lead named Bess. While working in baggage, all three of them played on their phones while I screening bags alone. AJ and Steffon finally alternated using the same table, instead of using one of the several open tables, and even argued which of them screened more bags. The two of them combined had not completed a fifth of what I did. Bess did absolutely no work. One of the passengers was a bit late, arriving when everybody else was already on the plane. He had one of those school lunch size chocolate milk cartons, which being over the allowable size limit, had to be thrown in the trash. Once the passenger was gone, Bess took the milk from the trash and drank it in the middle of the screening checkpoint, where airport staff, cameras, and even the passenger from the plane, as the windows in the checkpoint were very large and the plane was next to the building, could see her

Speaking of taking passenger's items, an Alaska airlines agent would take items from the trash after the flights left. She took unopened water bottles, toothpaste, and other items. Nil of course said nothing. We started taking the trash out earlier to prevent her from taking items. I'm sure over the years, thousands of items TSA has prohibited from flying has been taken by airport employees.

Back to AJ. When the lead promotion opened up, AJ assumed that as the "best" person in TSA history, and would of course be promoted. As I mentioned before, I was given the job without the AFSD even looking to see who else applied. AJ was furious when the announcement came out. Since had started at TSA just a mere five months before myself, he was more obviously more qualified.

When I was promoted to lead, I was on the opposite Deadhorse team of AJ.On the day my team arrived and his team left, AJ snuck a water bottle through the checkpoint, just to be an ass. He was last to board the plane and turned around and yelled "You missed this water bottle", then walked off. A TSA agent used his knowledge of the system to sneak an item on a plane, whether it was in his bag, or he hid it in the checkpoint ahead of time. Nil did nothing to stop this and AJ was not punished. On the day that my team would leave, I would put food in my backpack and a water bottle to drink at the airport. Ironically, two months in a row, I opened my bag on the plane to find a water bottle that went through TSA unseen.

AJ and I both returned to Fairbanks around the same time. One shift, there was only two members of leadership scheduled. I was supervisor in baggage. Since a supervisor is required in the passenger checkpoint at all times, I needed to work the checkpoint for an hour to cover lunch for the other supervisor. When I entered the checkpoint, AJ and an new officer he was training were holding a bag of a passenger. AJ informed me that a computer mouse had alarmed for explosives. The alarm required the passenger to receive a pat down, and have his bag searched. AJ told me the passenger had already received the pat down, and the bag had been cleared. The only thing left was for a supervisor to clear the mouse. After I cleared the mouse, the passenger went on his way and AJ said nothing. The next day Dan called me into his office. He had video of the passenger with the mouse pulled up on the monitor. He told me that AJ has sent an email to Donna that I had violated the screening procedure during that event. AJ claimed the passenger received a pat down from opting out of the body scanner, and not the pat down to resolve an alarm, which is different. Dan played the video, showing the passenger getting the pat down, the bag search, the alarm, the other supervisor talking to the passenger, and me showing up after all this happened. He said “well I don’t see a problem, you weren't even there”.

As much as I will write about Dan later, he was a good manager at one point, and he was correct. After leaving his officer, I assumed this was all over with. AJ wrote to Donna that I purposely skipped the procedure, which I didn't know because AJ lied to me about what happened before I arrived. For the incident, I received a letter of counseling which stated "I should ask more questions". Let's say you rent a car. The service agent tells you to take the blue car in spot number three. When you return to the rental agency, the manager tells you that you must pay $100 fee because you were supposed to take the red car in spot number four. When you tell the manager that the agent told you to take the blue, he tells you that you should have asked more questions. That's how stupid the letter from TSA was. Management could didn't even bother to ask the officer in training what happened, just just accepted with AJ's word. If their response was ask more questions, they acknowledge AJ withheld information, and purposely allowed a passenger to fly without proper screening. Nothing happened to AJ over this incident.

Both AJ and Steffon actively searched for drugs, despite the fact doing so is against policy. When doing a bag search an officer has to be the least invasive as possible. This means only going for the item selected during X-ray screening, and any items in the way. AJ and Steffon would look through the entire bag, thinking finding drugs made them heroic or relevant. The truth is, if any drugs are discovered in an improper manner, then the passenger can take TSA to court and win as demonstrated by Leb. On two separate occasions, while assigned to watch the exit only lane, AJ failed to notice an unscreened passenger walk right past him. Despite the mentioned above, AJ was eventually promoted to lead.

Once AJ became lead, he had the power trip that's all too common at TSA. One night I was assigned to the checkpoint with Francine. AJ was assigned to baggage. AJ came up to the checkpoint and started bossing officers around. When an officer refused to do as AJ wanted, the two took the matter to Francine. I moved closer to observe the situation. When AJ stated that people weren't doing as he told them, Francine politely told him, "Brandon and I are covering the checkpoint, we have it handled, you're supposed to be in baggage". AJ didn't like this answer and threatened to go to the manager. AJ made good on his word and called manager Dick. Francine received a write up for as Dick put it "not mentoring AJ", which is complete crap. Francine should not work for TSA, as her job knowledge is well below average, her communication and teamwork skills are nonexistent, and she refuses to do work. She handled this situation in the best possible way, but she went against Donna's golden child and lost.

One night, an officer called me over to deal with a passenger who refused to surrender Gatorade. When I told the passenger she couldn't bring large liquids with her, she said "I'm related to AJ, he's a boss here". I later found out the passenger is his mother-in-law. I almost laughed in her face when she said that. AJ has the same job title as me, a lead officer, which is only one step above entry level. In Fairbanks alone, the chain of command has three levels above lead officer, and nowhere near being a "boss". I also found it amusing she tried to intimidate me into allowing her to bring items through. When I told her the Gatorade is too large and not flying, she immediately went a different route and said she needed the drink for medical reasons. AJ of course told her to say this because medical items have no size limits. When I questioned how the drink was medicinal she replied that she needed it to take with her prescription medication. When I asked her to show me the prescription medication, she told me she had them in her checked luggage. I then asked her if she had any documentation at all to show she needed it for medical reasons. She had no documentation to support her claim. I didn't allow her to take the Gatorade through the checkpoint. It's no surprise that the best story somebody related to AJ could come up with was she needed the drink to use with an item that she didn't have. It's reasonable to assume that at some point since TSA was created, that at least one officer allowed prohibited items because they know the person.

AJ was eventually promoted to supervisor in Kentucky I believe. I'm not 100% on that, but it sounds right, so that's what I'll go with. I would like to take thank TSA management in Kentucky as one or more individuals recognized AJ for what he is. AJ failed his performance review as a supervisor and was busted down to officer and stripped of all leadership duties. This is proof that some TSA employees are not as incompetent as the mass of blue appears. After AJ was demoted, he crawled back to Fairbanks like the dog he is, and to the safety of FSD Donna.

Steffon was promoted to lead as well. He lacks the ability to think for himself, has no communication or people skills, and fails to adapt to changing events. While on the floor, the checkpoint is confused and slow, with no coordination. Steffon also lacks respect from the officers, which probably comes from him constantly calling officers his subordinates.

One night I was training a new hire. The new hire was conducting a pat down on a passenger in a wheelchair for the first time. The new hire was of course nervous and he was going at a slower pace to ensure he did the procedures correctly. Even though he was going slow, the passenger wasn't complaining. Despite this, Kevin who was the supervisor, approached me and said I needed to help him pat down the passenger to speed up the process. I refused to do as Kevin asked and he stormed off. Imagine how bad it looks and how the embarassed the passenger would feel if two officers did the pat down at the same time. Since I have to watch every screening procedure the new hire conducts, it would be a violation if I had to look away to help.

The first time I went to Deadhorse as a lead, the team I joined had already been there for two days. When I got off the plane the officers were already screening the passengers getting on. It wasn't until later that I had thought about it, but they had been screening with no leadership. Nil was at the other other terminal with her team. In fact, they had screened multiple flights with no leadership, which is a violation. The first thing I noticed upon entering the checkpoint was an officer named Sonya conducting a bag search. She did everything wrong from start to finish. I made her redo the procedure, and later showed her the correct procedure in the SOP. She was confused and asked how long that procedure had been in effect. The procedure had been in effect since I joined TSA a year earlier. Given the nature of TSA, and the fact that the procedure involved testing for explosives, I assume much longer than that. I asked Sonya how long she worked for

TSA. She replied it had been six years. I told her the procedure has probably been in effect that entire time.

Over the next three months, I witnessed several other violations committed by Sonya including improper checked baggage screening. When I confronted her about the checked baggage violation, she lied about it. I informed Nil each time I witnessed a violation and each was well documented. Sonya was put on a performance improvement plan and sent back to her home airport of Anchorage.

Nil showed me Sonya's performance review from the prior year. It was conducted by supervisor Kevin, the same Kevin as mentioned from the wheelchair incident earlier. Her review stated she was very knowledgeable with all procedures. Given what I witnessed, I would say Kevin never watched Sonya work. Instead sitting in the office giving out good reviews to avoid the hassle of accurate evaluations.

Officer Uma possessed terrible job knowledge. When Uma was corrected, she becomes defensive and argumentative. Once, after showing her the correct procedure in the SOP, she said to me, "that's wrong". She was unable to accept it and wanted to whine to the supervisor. When Roach, the supervisor showed her the SOP again, and told Uma she was wrong, Uma still refused to accept it. Uma then wanted to talk with the manager. We called Dan in Fairbanks, who looked it up himself and corrected her for third time. Uma wanted to take it higher, unwilling to accept she was wrong. Roach told Uma she was done playing this game and to drop it.

Pat joined the Deadhorse team a few months after I did. Twice in Fairbanks he fell asleep at the job. Instead of firing him, TSA management moved him the the Deadhorse rotation.

One of ours tasks was recording the time a plane would pull away from the building. Often we would be in the office while the plane was about 50 feet away. When the engines would start up and the plane taxied, Pat would walk into the supervisor office and would yell, "the plane is leaving" and what time it was. Pat apparently thought he was the only one aware the plane was leaving. Despite the the fact he had to yell over the noise it made, and the wind was coming through the open window blowing papers off the desk.

Pat was later fired after getting a passenger's name of a bag he screened. He sent her a sexual message through facebook. When Nil broke the news of the firing to a few of us, she attempted to be funny and said "your least favorite person has been fired". Two of us shouted "Uma", obviously not what Nil expected. She then said "your second least favorite person". Both of us said a little less enthusiastic "Pat". Nil later told me that after Pat had his job interview, he was sent to get a psychiatric review. This is a red flag, as I've never heard of any other TSA officer having to do that before being hired. Another fun fact, that was confidential information, which Nil had no right to share with me. Nil gave me information on numerous occasions that I should not have known.

Once, when an officer took some time off, a fellow named Cordy from Anchorage was slotted to fill the shift. He was one of those people who's done everything and attempts to one up everybody else. Cordy apparently owns three planes and has been on half a dozen humanitarian trips to underdeveloped countries. While working at TSA in Dallas, he claims to have discovered one of the largest drug shipments smuggled onto a plane. He claims to have found the drugs after U.S. Customs and Border agents already screened the plane. He claims his report was on the desk of the President of the United States the very next day.

While screening one flight, several passengers were late, so one officer had to stay in the checked baggage area to screen the late bags. This left us with three people, one to check tickets, I was at the metal detector, and Cordy was on X-ray. Cordy called a bag check. Since our fourth officer was busy he had to conduct the search himself. He completely skipped the explosive detection step. While looking for the item of interest he started handing everything he removed from the bag back to the passenger. For those of you that have had a bag searched, TSA makes a point to tell you not to touch anything until they're finished. Without verifying he found the correct item, Cordy could have handed a prohibited to a passenger. When I showed Cordy the correct procedure in the SOP, he said that since he was assigned to X-ray and not bag search, he didn't have to follow the SOP. After he said that, I asked him "are you fucking stupid?". Which even though it's the correct response, for the government full of whiny incompetent morons, it's the wrong response. When Cordy got written up, he complained about my remark. Nil asked me "Stumpe, did you say that?". I said yep and she asked why. I responded, because he is. Nil nodded her head in agreement and replied, "yeah well you can't say it though." I got my slap on the wrist and moved on.

When Cordy eventually came to Fairbanks, Stoak actually said something along the same lines to him Stoak got fired. Stoak was worthless and should've been gone long before. I got a an undocumented warning and Stoak was fired. One major difference was when I did it, it was during a one on one conversation, and Stoak said it in front of other people. When I made the remark I was in favor with management, and they let it slip. Stoak was disliked by management, and this was a convenient way to fire him. On a side note, a passenger commented "this guy is fucking annoying", after Cordy followed two passengers around, yapping.

The X-ray machine in Deadhorse is old and outdated. Like many TSA officers. The X-ray has only one screen, instead of the usual two. This makes recognizing items much more difficult. Before an officer worked in Deadhorse for the first time, they would take a computer simulated test, which in no way resembles the real machine. Passing the test would certified officers on a machine they've never even seen. Nil would have me watch new officers to see if they were ready or needed help. One officer from Anchorage missed a fictional bow and arrow. Instead of learning from her mistake, she instead told me it was my fault as the monitor, since I didn't do it for her. I refused to pass her on the X-ray, so I passed it to Nil.

An officer named Poe was operating the X-ray machine and I happened to glance at the screen. I noticed the image of a knife, in the very backpack that was exiting the tunnel and being grabbed by the owner. I quickly informed the passenger I need to look in his bag and tool control of it. During the search, I discovered the knife in the side pocket of the backpack. It was right on top as I unzipped the pocket. I told put the bag back into the X-ray to have the image reexamined. While I was explaining to the passenger that he would be unable to carry his knife onto the plane, his bag came out of the X-ray and he grabbed it. He then dug to the bottom of the same pocket and pulled out a second knife and asked "what about this?" I was in complete disbelief. I took control of the second knife, and went to the X-ray to view the image. Sure enough, with the first knife removed, the second knife became visible in the bag. Poe missed two seperate knives, in the exact same area just moments apart.

One month, I took two days off at the beginning of the rotation to Deadhorse. My leave was approved weeks in advance. When I flew up on Monday, I discovered that Nil was not there. The manager of Deadhorse, who was out of Anchorage, made Nil and the supervisor from the other rotation do mandatory training in Anchorage. The other rotation had two leads. One of them could have stayed two extra days to keep leadership present as was required. Instead, TSA in Deadhorse screened flights for two days with no supervision and no officers certified to clear explosive alarms. Not only was this a huge violation, that could easily have been corrected, but it was completely ignored by management.

Upon returning to work at Fairbanks, working with more officers equals more problems. One officer, Jay did not get along with another officer who was always oddly cheerful. Jay was in the break room one day playing with his pocket knife. With his knife in hand, Jay said, “I'm going to slit her throat”, naming the officer he didn’t like. She wanted to go the police, but the manager, Dick talked her out of it. Donna and Dick didn’t want the situation to leave TSA, even though it was a serious death threat and should have been treated as such. TSA management fired Jay and swept the situation under the rug, preferring not to deal with issue.

An officer by the name of Alvah was constantly late, missed prohibited items on X-ray, and had appalling job knowledge. He put in a transfer request to move to California and while waiting for approval Alvah committed several violations. When I asked Nil if Alvah would receive disciplinary action, she said that if written up, Alvah’s transfer would be denied and he would stay in Fairbanks. Nil stated “It would be better for us if he left”. Alvah got off the hook merely because management didn’t want to deal with him. and he’s free to continue making the same mistakes, which instead of being fired, could be simple warning.

A passenger approached me one night from the screened area of the airport. He was holding a ziplock bag filled with a dozen bullets. He told me that he was sitting at the gate and noticed the bullets were still in his bag and he didn't want to get into trouble. After asking the passenger a few questions and reviewing tape, I discovered that the officer on X-ray was Hank, an officer who had been with TSA for less than a year. I asked the passenger which pocket the bullets were in, and if I could borrow his bag to recreate the X-ray image. There was no mistaking the bullets in the bag, and nothing to block the view. When the Dick and I reviewed the situation with Hank, all he would say is "I don't know how I missed it". Had the passenger not worried about the bullets, we would have never known they escaped detection.

Another time, an item on the X-ray screen appeared to be a firearm part. As a supervisor has to deal with firearm related items, I took the bag to the search table. When the passenger approached, I said "it looks like you have a firearm part in your bag". He casually replied "yeah, they looked at it before also". Firearm parts are not allowed to be carried on the plane. He just said that somebody already looked at it and let it go. My first thought was he came through earlier in the morning, had gone out to smoke and was now returning. When I asked him when he had come through, he said that he was scheduled to fly out the night before. His flight was cancelled, so he was rebooked. I informed him the item would not be allowed through and then asked him what time he was screened the night before. After reviewing footage, I discovered that the night shift officer had pulled the bag for a search. While the officer was looking through the bag, he pulled out a small cloth sack, which contained the firearm part. He did not look through the cloth sack at all. When he couldn't find the part, he sent the bag through the X-ray again. The officer left the cloth sack at the table, and when the second X-ray image didn't show a firearm part, he just accepted that an item can magically disappear, and let everything go. The half assed, give up easy work ethic is common in TSA.

The two incidents above were caught by random luck. They prove that numerous dangerous items go undiscovered and are carried onto aircraft all the time.

Both officers in the previous events were gone within several weeks after each event. The next case, when compared with the previous two occurrences, shows the corruption of TSA management and how they exercise favoritism. I had a bag search on a passenger with a large liquid. I told the passenger she couldn't carry the item on the aircraft. She replied "I've already been through here with it". After investigating, I discovered the previous officer who searched it was none other than supervisor Nil. Nil looked at the item and gave it back to the passenger. When I told Dick, he questioned Nil about it and she replied, "Oh, I didn't think about it". Nil received no warning or disciplinary action, despite the fact that unlike the previous two cases, she had the prohibited item in her hand, and gave it back. It could be argued that it's just a liquid, and the other two items were firearm components. While that is true, TSA has the liquid ban for a viable reason, it's because of the existence of liquid explosive. The difference between the two officers and Nil, Nil worked ten plus years at TSA with the members of Fairbanks management, and she was a supervisor.

Supervisor Francine has practical no job knowledge. On multiple occasions she called for the wrong screening procedures to be conducted, especially after explosive alarms. After correcting Francine, I would inform management of her poor performance. They obviously spoke to her, because she was telling people I was targeting her, but management never took any action to correct the issue. Every other supervisor, no matter how lazy, or terribly they performed their job, would at least work on occasion. During the five years I worked at TSA, Francine would only ever leave the comfort of her desk to take a break. Any time there was a supervisor call, she would make eye contact with the lead and give the "you take care of it look". She never helped with opening or closing the checkpoint, usually hiding in the breakroom.

When I was hired there was a lead named Minda. She failed her lead review, and was demoted down to officer. Minda made so many mistakes that she was put on a performance improvement plan. She spent over a year, A YEAR, being watched by another officer, constantly making mistakes, before TSA fired her. Over $40,000 was paid to her while TSA paid another officer to babysit her.

TSA has a policy that family members or officers in relationships can't hold authority over each other. This has caused siblings and spouses to work different shifts upon promotion. Fairbanks however chooses when to exercise this policy. Dick had a brother in law who was an officer working directly beneath him. He showed clear favoritism toward this officer. They were allowed to continue to work together despite the conflict of interest.

When the BDO program was disbanded in Fairbanks, the officers were given several options. They could transfer as BDOs to other airports were the program was still active, or they would be given a position of a similar pay grade at any airport with an opening. Two Fairbanks BDOs chose to remain. One was made a lead, and turned out to be a terrible lead It makes sense to TSA to put an employee in a leadership role merely because there position disappeared. The other former BDO, Daryll, eventually ended up in an office position, which I'll cover later on. Before Daryll moved to the office, he worked as an officer in several positions such as ticket checker and exit monitor. He spent a tremendous amount of time complaining, even though he only performed the easy tasks. As a BDO he did very little to no actual work. He was also insubordinate, refusing to do work when a supervisor asked him. Daryll was never punished, because he's friends with Donna. Had most officers acted the way he had, they would have been fired.

TSA has made several changes to the SOP over the years. One change dealt with using a specific X-ray machine. If a laptop was in a bag, the search officer can run the explosive test on the laptop without sending the laptop or the bag back through the X-ray. I guess the reasoning behind this is to save time, however it opens up a huge hole in security. Laptops are easy to open and modify the interior. For this reason laptops are considered high risk for concealment. Laptops also are made of metal and electronics, and must be removed from the bag because they can block the view of other items in the bag and vice versa.

Even after the policy change, I still ran laptops through the X-ray again. Once, while waiting for the bag and laptop, I noticed a knife in the bag that could not be seen because the laptop was obscuring it. The officer didn't notice the knife. I stopped him and pointed it out. I was disappointed, because I thought he was one of the better X-ray operators we had. Had I not sent the property through the X-ray, the knife would have passed through undetected. This method could be used to smuggle many different items through checkpoints, because TSA thinks it's being progressive, In reality, the attempt to save a few seconds of screening time opens up more vulnerabilities.

Time abuse was another issue in Fairbanks. Most officers in Fairbanks work ten hour shifts with an hour lunch. Some officers worked eight hour shifts with a two hour split. Officers with the hour lunch were not required to clock out. From the time they walked away from the checkpoint, they had exactly one hour to be back. The officers working the split were required to clock out for their two hour split.

Two officers abused the time. Instead of clocking in and out at the checkpoint like they were supposed to do. They would use the time machine in the break room. The problem was, they would use the bathroom, buy food, put winter clothes on, make phone calls, or do whatever else they wanted before and after they made a time punch. These officers would be absent for up to two hours and 15 minutes. When I took this issue to Dan, he looked at the time punches. Since the punches were two hours apart, he did nothing. I continued to bring up the issue, but Dan shrugged it off and said "Donna's looking into the matter". Many officers who were a minute late from lunch were scolded, but these two were not. This is another example of how TSA chooses when they want to enforce rules or ignore rules if it's a bother to them.

During one shift, I learned that a used explosive initiator had been discovered while I was acting supervisor. I was informed an hour after the passenger had left the screening area. Upon discovery the initiator, the screening officer turned to Dan, who was standing near the search table. Dan confiscated the item, but required no additional screening for the passenger. This was one of four components that makes up a bomb. Upon discovering one of these components, the passenger will receive multiple screening procedures and questioning before being allowed to fly. To be fair, Dan probably noticed some elderly passengers to harass and didn't have time to worry about explosives. Dan received no disciplinary action for this incident. Being friends with the Federal Security Director doesn't hurt. Everybody can rest easy knowing management prefers to cover each others asses over ensuring proper protocol. Not only was I furious, but so was Glenn. As the explosive expert, Glenn is supposed to inspect the item, and he's the only person in Fairbanks who can clear an explosive.

In Fairbanks, we had two breach incidents that highlight the confusion and lack of communication at TSA. One passenger walked up the exit only stairs. When a breach occurs, police and management must be notified immediately. The lead in charge at the time, happend to be a displaced BDO, thus gifted, not earning the leadership position. The notifications were never made. Management only became aware of the event three hours later when the supervisor finally showed up to the checkpoint and was informed by the lead.

The second incident was a planned drill by Glenn. Glenn asked a member of the air force named Mike, to walk past security to test the reaction. To avoid confusion management and airport police were informed of the drill. When Mike breached security, the supervisor immediately followed him toward the gates. A newly promoted lead went in search of the incident book to look up the procedures. If you're reviewing the procedures during the incident, it's too late.

I got on the phone and called the airport police and then Dan. I could see the the event while on the phone describing the events to Dan. When the police officer showed up, she told the Mike to stop and get on the ground. When Mike didn't comply, she drew her weapon. Even with the weapon pointed at him and the repeated shouts to get on the ground, Mike remained standing. When I informed Dan the a weapon was drawn and Mike wasn't complying, he began to worry. Since this is a drill for TSA, an airport police officer shouldn't be using a weapon. Greg was hiding near a gate and came out yelling drill repeatedly. It was lucky Greg was by the gate, because he usually hides further from the drill location to avoid being seen. The airport police officer knew a drill would be run, but TSA failed to notify them it was starting. The reason Mike didn't get on the ground was he had a bad leg and he couldn't get down. This situation could have ended in disaster.

Chapter 4

Other Airports

You don’t have to work at TSA to know sometimes they are absolutely doing things wrong. Knowing the correct procedures sure helps to identify those mistakes. This chapter incidents I noticed while traveling through other airports.

The first two events took place before I worked for TSA. Traveling for vacation while I was still in high school, my mother placed her shoes on the X-ray belt. Only one of her shoes came out of the other side. As many people might have noticed, the X-ray has heavy lead curtains to prevent the radiation from escaping. Often lightweight objects will get stuck and require a heavier item or person to help push them through. When my mother asked the X-ray officer where her other shoe had gone, she replied “you only came in with one shoe”, and turned away. My mother looked at her in disbelief and said “why would I only have one shoe when I have two feet?”. A second officer gave the first officer the “are you stupid look”, walked over to the X-ray entry tunnel and pushed it in. When the first officer saw the image, she gave a small chuckle and said “oh now I see the other shoe”.

The second event happened when I traveled through the Louis Armstrong New Orleans International Airport. As I approached the TSA checkpoint I was surprised to find no line. Instead of walking all the way around to the start of the line, I ducked under the rope right next to the ID check. The officer looked at me and said “you have to start from the beginning of the line”. I turned around and there was nobody in line. I looked at him, he was dead serious and I said no. He waited for a few seconds, and finally looked at my ID and ticket. He was just trying to use what small amount of authority he had to be an asshole and make himself feel better.

As I mentioned before, there is the playbook team that conducts screening away from the checkpoint. At both Los Angeles International and Seattle–Tacoma International Airport, I witnessed playbook teams at gates using their personal phones. I watched both groups. The Los Angeles officers checked the ID of one person, of the dozens that passed them, while the Seattle team never even looked away from their phones. These are not isolated incidents, and most likely happen across the entire country on a daily basis. TSA spends millions of dollars a year, to pay officer to stand around on their phones.

When I worked at Deadhorse, the trip home consisted of a three hour layover in Anchorage. A Fairbanks talked about how the Anchorage officers skipped screening procedures. One day, while waiting for the flight to Fairbanks, I decided to go through the security checkpoint and get a pat down to see how bad it could be. The officer who conducted the pat down was a lead, and later I found out a trainer, when he signed documents for Fairbanks new hires. I remember because he’s the brother of a Fairbanks employee who was paid for the five years I worked there, but i’m certain never actually did work. He was the copy/paste scheduling guy before we merged with Anchorage, and he didn't have a job title for a year after that. Back to the pat down, it was half assed, would have failed the yearly testing requirements. He was so clueless he wouldn't have noticed if I had a cat hidden in my shirt. This demonstrates, that on a daily basis, thousands of items could be smuggled through TSA, because of lazy, incompetent officers.

I traveled through the Seattle–Tacoma International Airport about a week before the Seahawks and the Broncos played the Super Bowl. I was standing in line for the scanner, when one of the officers shouted "Broncos" and pointed to a passenger behind me. The passenger was wearing a Broncos shirt. The officer who shouted, and two other officers, including the X-ray operator, all stopped what they were doing, and pointed at the person and loudly went "OOOOOOOOOHHHHHHHHHHHHHHHHHH", like a bunch of children. It was completely unprofessional, and held up the entire screening process. The scanner line was moving slowly, and while I was waiting, the officer who started the the chant held up my bag and asked "who's is this?" When I told him it was mine, I started to take a step toward him, he said "no go ahead and stay in line". Violation number one, property must be searched at the search table with the passenger present. He conducted the search by the X-ray. I watched as he pulled out my dvd case. I understand this process as disks show the same color as explosives. I've searched hundreds of disks in Fairbanks, due to officers who can't tell the difference between a bomb and a movie.

Violation number two, he didn't conduct the explosive testing on my property. After I cleared the scanner, I packed my items and looked around for any leadership. I was amazed, though I guess I shouldn't have been, to discover not a single lead or supervisor in sight. In the back right of the checkpoint, was an open door. I peeked my head inside to find two supervisor and a lead sitting in the office, two of them eating food. No wonder the officers conducted themselves are terrible, the leadership had no oversight and eats instead of works. I said "excuse me, there's a problem". One of the supervisors looked at me and said "yes?". I relayed the story of the Bronco shirt, then mentioned how my bag wasn't screening properly. The supervisor, not knowing I worked for TSA said "I don't see a problem". I replied with "My item was searched because it's organic, meaning the X-ray operator believe it could be explosives, and the search officer didn't run a test for explosives, how stupid it that?" She looked confused, until I said "It's also part of the SOP". She rudely asked what airport I worked at and then got up to go speak with the officers. At this point, I was still there with my property. The supervisor could have had the proper test conducted, instead she said nothing, so I walked off. Complete failure for TSA Seattle

In the Los Angeles security line two officers checking IDs, however only one had a UV light. The officer who checked my ID, a driver's license from Alaska, did so without checking any of the security features. Every state has different security features. When checking IDs, TSA officers are required to use the UV light, or at least magnification to verify the ID is real. The officer looked at my ID for about two seconds, apparently was well trained enough to tell it was real, and let me go. Using the UV light would have taken only seconds longer, but TSA can't bother to do the job correctly.

Further in the checkpoint, I noticed the passenger if front of my didn't receive the required explosive test. When I informed the supervisor about what happened, she immediately got up and ran over to the officers as fast as she could. Even though the officers in LA can't bother to do the job right, at least the supervisor was willing to fix the mistake. Though it might have been because I informed her I worked for TSA.

San Francisco has a private security force. While technically not TSA, they are required to follow TSA guidelines, and pretty much look and act like TSA. I was at the international security lane of the San Francisco International Airport. The line for the scanner was incredibly long. The officer at the scanner asked the next person to step forward. The officer tried to show the person how to stand correctly, when another person entered the scanner. The two passengers were an older couple that spoke no english, and were confused about the process. Since they didn't understand, the officer began yelling at them "ONLY ONE PERSON AT A TIME". The officer yelled several times, until another passenger said, "I don't think they speak english, yelling isn't going to help". When I finally got through the scanner and was waiting for my property, I noticed the lead and supervisor, some twenty feet from the scanner, laughing at each other. They had no awareness or didn't care what happened around them. To be fair, they were probably also dipshits and would have yelled at people who don't understand them either.

I was traveling on vacation with my wife and year old daughter. Large liquids are allowed for infants, but are required to undergo explosive testing. Knowing the procedure I removed the liquids out of my bag. Baby foods and yogurt are included in the liquid category. Screening methods vary for different items. In Fairbanks, the officer tested the liquids took only a few minutes and we were on our way.

Anchorage is about a 45 minute flight from Fairbanks. In Anchorage we had to leave the secure area to deal with our bags. We went through the TSA line, less than two hours after going through Fairbanks. We had the exact same items but the screening experience was completely different. The liquids got pulled, I went to the search table, and the officer told me I needed a pat down and all my bags would be searched. It doesn't take a TSA agent who knows the procedures to figure out that something it wrong if two different airports are conducting different screening. I asked to speak to a supervisor. A lead officer came over. He was four foot nothing, so I'll call him Frodo. Frodo said the exact same thing, I would need a pat down and have my bags search. I told him, no that's the procedure if I had different liquids. Frodo still insisted I needed the screening done. I then told him exactly what was in the SOP, why he was wrong with my items, and asked him to check.

The SOP is readily available to all officers to ensure the correct screening is conducted. It would have taken him moments only to verify the procedure. Frodo refused to look up the correct procedure, and said "I'm the lead, what I say goes". At this point, I had been a lead for four years, leads definitely can't force people through extra screening.. I asked him to get the supervisor, who I could see sitting at the desk. Frodo refused, and since this was going nowhere because he's an idiot, I went through the screening. Frodo's lack of knowledge, and laziness resulted in me getting a pat down and waiting twenty minutes in screening.

TSA states that it tries to be as minimally invasive as possible, yet I received a pointless pat down. How many millions of times has TSA forced people to receive extra screening because they have terrible job knowledge? I made an inquiry about the different screening methods on the TSA website. The response I got was, "The SOP can be open for interpretation by local officers". We know TSA wants consistency among all airports, thus requiring a centralized training academy. Even more ridiculous, do they really expect people to believe, that a government security agency, their sole purpose is to prevent terrorism and thwart lives lost, would devise procedures that allow any officer to alter the screening to their desire? That is damn stupid.

On our return trip home. Having already spent twenty hours traveling halfway around the world, I forgot to take the liquids out of my bag. I realized my mistake as my bag went into the X-ray at the Anchorage checkpoint. I was surprised to see my bag cleared without the need to be searched. When I looked to see who was on X-ray, I was amused to see it was Frodo himself. The little guy didn't even see the oversized liquids, which are required to be removed and screened. I chuckled at the irony of Frodo missing the items. I received three different screening methods for the same items, and TSA preaches consistency.

Chapter 5

My fight against TSA

It began with the office of investigation (OOI) came to Alaska. They interviewed officers in both Fairbanks and Anchorage. During my interview, I relayed to the investigator the local issues with supervision and management. I was not alone. Many Fairbanks officers reported the same supervisors and managers. With Fairbanks management under the scope, the OOI forward the complaints to Ryan in Anchorage.

As the head of Alaska TSA, it fell to Ryan to resolve the issues. He sent an email to every member of TSA Alaska. The email stated the recent OOI visit revealed Alaska is doing very well, with only a few minor issues. This was contradictory to what Fairbanks officers had reported. After several months Ryan did nothing to resolve the issues. It was clear he didn't care. TSA Fairbanks made an official complaint through the union.

The union leader was Dara, a Fairbanks officer. Now Ryan was forced to act, instead of sweeping in under the rug. Ryan sent his Assistant Federal Security Director (AFSD) Puffy to Fairbanks to investigate. Puffy interviewed the officers again, the main concern being leadership problems. I told him about the multiple violations, the laziness, and lack of job knowledge among supervisors, and management. Puffy promised to hold leadership accountable and clean up Fairbanks.

Puffy appeared to make good on the promises when he began interviewing the supervisors. What happened next was the complete opposite. Puffy and newly promoted manager LeRoach asked me to write a statement about Dara. In fact, LeRoach told be specific things to write about Dara. I told them I can't write a statement about things I don't know, regarding a person who works different hours. I later found out they asked other officers to write statements about Dara also. Instead of addressing the union complaint, Puffy was attempting to remove Dara. Several weeks later I was told I was under investigation and the person who ordered it was Puffy.

Every quote used in this chapter comes from official written statements regarding my case.One of the allegations, checking a text in the office has been done by most officers. I was also accused of bullying two officers. One officer was if I had ever bullied him, and he responded that I had not. The second officer was never even spoken too. Had a proper investigation been done, both officers would have been interview and asked to write statements. I however spoke to the second officer, and received a written statement from that officer. The officer's statement reads "LTSO Stumpe never bullied me. Ever since I have worked for TSA he has trained me and encouraged me to grow by challenging me to think for myself instead of just giving me answers.

On October 24th 2016, I made a mistake while screening. I conducted the wrong explosive test on a bag of sand. On December 17th 2016, I was removed from screening functions, the primary reasoning being a bag search where I missed a screening procedure. TSA claims I purposely let the item go without proper screening. In fact I made an honest mistake. An officer named Beele noticed and told me about my mistake later, but the passenger had already left. In his statement, Beele claimed he told me while the passenger was still present in the checkpoint. Video footage shows my mistake, followed by the passenger packing his bag. The footage never shows Beele speaking to me. With over a dozen time stamped cameras in the checkpoint, why is the footage of Beele speaking to me absent?

It was seven weeks from the incident until I was removed from screening duties. During those seven weeks, I trained three officers, including a newly promoted lead and a supervisor who transfered from Seattle. When I pointed this fact out during my reply to the charge, Donna's response was

"The decision to remove him from screening came after a monthly meeting with management in Anchorage, the removal was suggested by Puffy".

This means one of two things. Fairbanks management understood is was a mistake, but when Puffy found out and used it to remove me. Or Fairbanks management believed my actions were intentional and waited seven weeks to discuss removing me from screening. During those seven weeks, I could potentially allow much worse things to happen. However TSA tries to spin it, it was handled poorly.

Since I was unable to perform screening functions, I was assigned by management to load the X-ray machine in checked baggage. The only thing I did for several weeks was putting bags on the X-ray belt. That changed the day I witnessed a violation committed by Donna and Dan, the top two ranking members of management in Fairbanks.

On January 2nd 2017 we were very busy and had an officer in training. I noticed the uncertified officer screening bags without a monitor, which is a violation. When I informed Dan of the situation, he paid it no mind and said "we got it covered." His claim was contradictory to what I saw, so I decided to review it. While watching the footage, I noticed the officer in training had screened four bags without proper supervision. Due to several large international flights, Donna and Dan were helping to move bags. Both Donna and Dan handed bags to the officer, and Dan even stood by the officer during screening. Dan is not certified and can't monitor officers in training. I figured management would deny any wrongdoing, and remove my access to the cameras. So before confronting management I went to officers I trusted. A supervisor named Tad An officer named Karla and a former supervisor named Marl. I showed them the footage and got written statements.

When I provided the information to Dan, he denied the violation. Dan said "there was a moment where no monitor was watching the officer". When I presented statements from three officers, including myself, to management, Puffy responded with "I looked into the matter, and there was no violation". The day after I reported the violation, I was told to report only to the office, and no longer to the airport.

I spent my final six weeks working for TSA in the office. At first I was assigned to inventory the warehouse and fill the order for new supplies. The warehouse was a mess. Nothing was organized and trash littered the floor. When I gave the order form to Daryl, he looked surprised that I left off small and XXL gloves. I told him not only are there hundreds of boxes of both but neither get used. TSA wastes money stockpiling supplies it doesn't use because people are too lazy and stupid to inventory correctly. Ordering 20 boxes of everything requires no work.

While at the office I was cast aside. I spend most of my time reading books and playing games on my phone while collecting $25 an hour. The office staff was barely visible. I sat by the door, and could see every person entering and leaving. Daryl told me he was going for coffee, he was gone for an hour. The staff didn't have to clock in, they would show up late and leave early. One employee forgot something at home and took half and hour to retrieve the item. The TSA office staff has no accountability and takes full advantage of the circumstances. They did things uniformed officers would get disciplined or even fired for with no consequences.

During my six weeks at the office I received a proposed decision regarding the investigation against me. The proposal called for my removal from TSA. The following are quotes pulled directly from the proposed removal.

1)"I cannot say with certainty that your behavior was intentional"

2)"I considered your time in service with TSA of over five(5) years, the fact that your performance reviews indicate that you have at least met or exceeded expectations, and that fact that you have not received any prior discipline while a federal employee"

3)"I see no possibility for rehabilitation"

Given those statements, I fail to see how the proposing official decided removal was the best option. The failed screening was the main charge for removal. Several other charges they filed against me that make it more absurd. The second charge was that I acted unprofessionally after a X-ray machine broke. TSA provided one statement regarding my '"unprofessional behavior". One statement from half a dozen officers present at the time. I provided statements from three of the officers present.

1)"I don't specifically remember any negative behavior from LTSO Stumpe. However, I also know that if I did think something was inappropriate, I likely would have spoken to Brandon at the time"

2)"Then and now my recollection was that I did not personally witness any actions that were unprofessional"

3)"I personally would not consider his behavior to be unprofessional"

Remember TSA and math don't blend well. TSA management considered the statement of one individual as carrying more weight that the testimony of three individuals.

The last charge has to do with spreading false rumors. TSA claims that Dara the union leader, started a rumor and relayed it to me. TSA management wrote the following.

"I believe that Dara did in fact make the statement to you"

Dara was brought up on similar the same charge for spreading false rumors. I have a letter regarding Dara's case, stating the charges were dropped. If TSA claims Dara allegedly started the rumor but dropped the charges against her from lack of evidence. I see no reasonable explanation why the charge was a deciding factor in my removal.

The following statement is from a TSA Federal Security Director, obviously not from Alaska, in regards to a different investigation.

"In general, the proposing official is a management official within the employee's chain of supervision, while the deciding official is a management official in the employees chain of supervision higher than the proposing official. (Emphasis added). Simply because the employee has the title that allows his/her to function as a Deciding Official (DO) does not mean that it follows the requirements of this same policy, which requires the DO to be within the chain of supervision. I find this to be a misapplication of TSA MD 1100.75-3. Therefore, the DO in this case does not have authority to issue this Decision Notice. Accordingly, I also find that Management failed to follow Agency policy. Based on the foregoing, I dismiss all Charges in this matter."

That statement also refers to my case. My deciding official was not in my chain of command. TSA violated their own management directive to remove me. Why would they do that? The deciding official, reports directly to Puffy. It's a bit convenient that the person who wants me gone is the boss of the person who officially fired me. I have all the statements to back to my claims, including where the deciding official admits Puffy is his direct supervisor.

I was fired for "knowingly" violating screening procedures. Not only did I provide the violation by Dan and Donna, but I detailed two other violations that were not only intentional but completely ignored. Officer Beele committed the first violation. An officer approached me during a shift and informed me that Beele had allowed an oversized liquid through the checkpoint. Beele was on X-ray, he looked at the item, conducted no explosive testing and allowed it through. I asked the officer to write a statement, and provided it to Dan. The matter was never reviewed. Beele ended up writing the statement about my screening violation.

The second violation is probably the worst violation I have ever seen. It occurred when officer Flair was in checked baggage. Flair received an explosive alarm an a bag she was screening. As the supervisor, I responded to resolve the alarm. The bag had too much metal for the X-ray to see through. The procedure is then to visually and physically inspect the area and items which the view is blocked. This often required conducting explosive testing as well. The first thing I noticed about the bag Flair was screening is that the items appeared to be neatly packed and had no appearance of being disturbed. Most TSA officers cram the items back into the bag in the fastest way possible, especially officer Flair. I asked if she had removed all the items and inspected them, she replied yes. I screened all the items as if she never conducted the search, and performed the alarm clearing procedures. After I cleared the property, I had Flair repack the back, noting it was not as neat as when I removed the items. I reviewed footage of search which confirmed my suspicion and uncovered additional information. After Flair opened the bag, she is seen looking over her shoulder toward me. While I can't be seen in the footage, it's clear she's checking to see if i'm watching her. Instead of removing items, as she claimed, she used the explosive testing cloth on the top of the items she could see. That is improper screening. When she attempted to put the cloth into the machine to run the test, she dropped it on the floor by mistake. According to procedure, that cloth is considered contaminated and she is required to rescreen the items. Flair again looks to see if i'm watching her before testing the contaminated cloth. I informed Dan of the violation Flair committed, with video evidence that she intentionally skipped screening procedures.

The following day, I was reprimanded because officer Flair didn't change her contaminated gloves and didn't clean the contaminated search table after she repacked the bag. I was reprimanded for her mistakes because I was the supervisor in baggage, despite the fact that video shows I was not present when these violations happened. It's completely ridiculous i'm the one taking heat after noticing, collecting, and reporting a violation, which the officer lied about. An illegal item or explosive could easily have made it onto the aircraft because of Flairs incompetence.

In the above cases, neither officer was investigated, remediated, or removed from screening. TSA however came full assault on me for supposably committing the same violation. TSA management demonstrates a clear lack of consistency and targeting officers, allowing mediocracy.

A few months after I was fired, spoke to a friend still working for TSA. Officer Beele, the same officer would wrote the statement claiming I intentionally skipped the proper screening procedure.

He was promoted to my vacant lead position lead less than two months after I left. I won't touch that one, you get the idea.

These are the things I witnessed in five years at a small airport. Imagine what tens of thousands of employees over a dozen years have done. TSA is just an expensive security act full of corrupt management and poor quality officers. TSA will never be effective unless it receives a complete overhaul. If all the TSA officers that couldn't perform their job functions were fired, the handful of remaining officers would be burned out rather quickly, and air travel would probably be limited to several planes flying nationwide a day.

For a good laugh. Check out Key and Peele Al Qaeda meeting on Youtube.

www.ingramcontent.com/pod-product-compliance
Lightning Source LLC
Chambersburg PA
CBHW031325250726
48656CB00005B/1975
* 9 7 8 1 9 8 3 1 0 1 5 5 7 *